MATHS

TEN S to improve y
FRACTIONS
for ages 8-9

Step 1	Introducing halves and quarters	2
Step 2	Introducing thirds	6
Step 3	Introducing eighths	8
Step 4	Introducing tenths	10
Step 5	Halves and quarters of numbers	12
Step 6	Same-sized pieces, different fractions	16
Step 7	Using fractions	20
Step 8	Introducing mixed numbers	24
Step 9	Introducing decimals	26
Step 10	Using decimals	28
Parents' pages		30

AUTHOR Ian Gardner
ILLUSTRATOR George Turner

Let's learn at home

Step 1: Introducing halves and quarters

This step will help you to make and recognise shapes which are divided into halves ($\frac{1}{2}$) and quarters ($\frac{1}{4}$).

And when you share something into four equal amounts, we call those parts quarters.

Halving is when you share something into two equal amounts.

Divide each shape into two equal pieces. Shade the halves in different colours.

In each of the squares below, use a single line to divide the shape into two halves. Can you find eight different ways? The first one has been done for you.

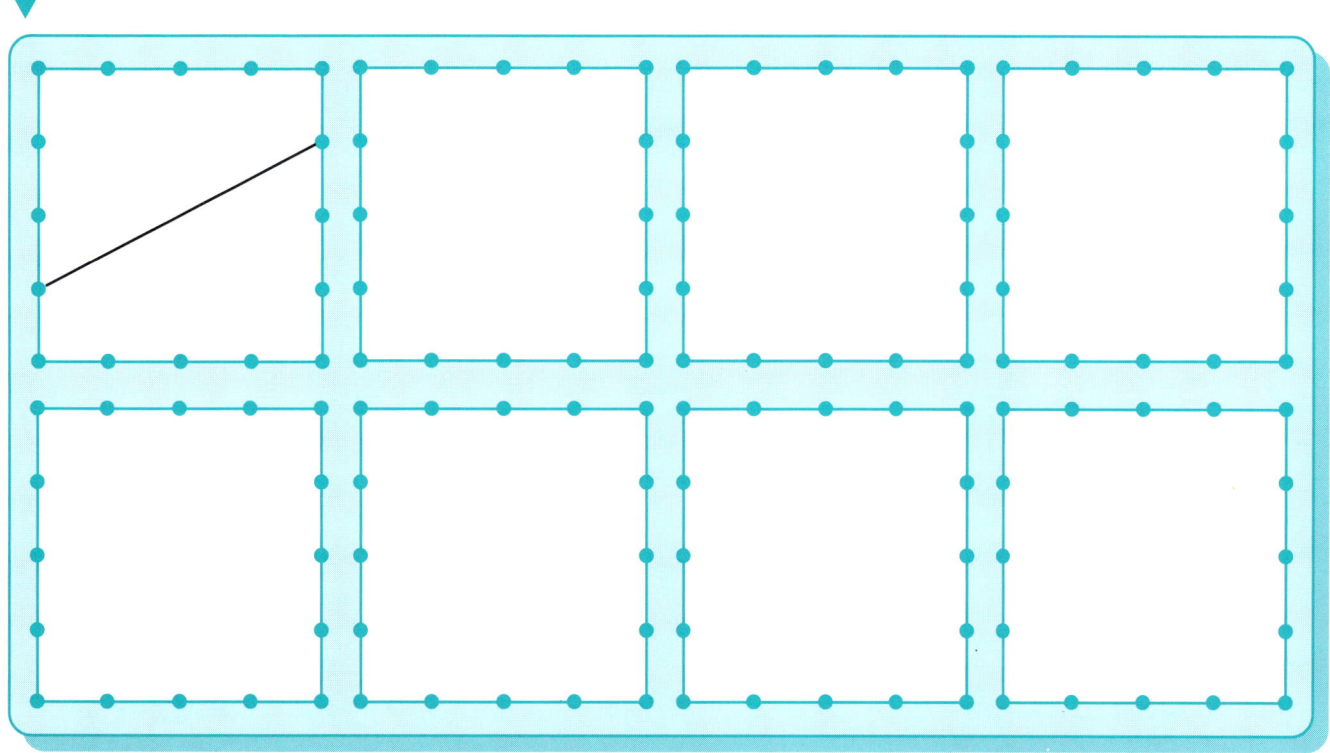

Look at these shapes. Have they been divided into halves? Mark each one with a ✓ or ✗.

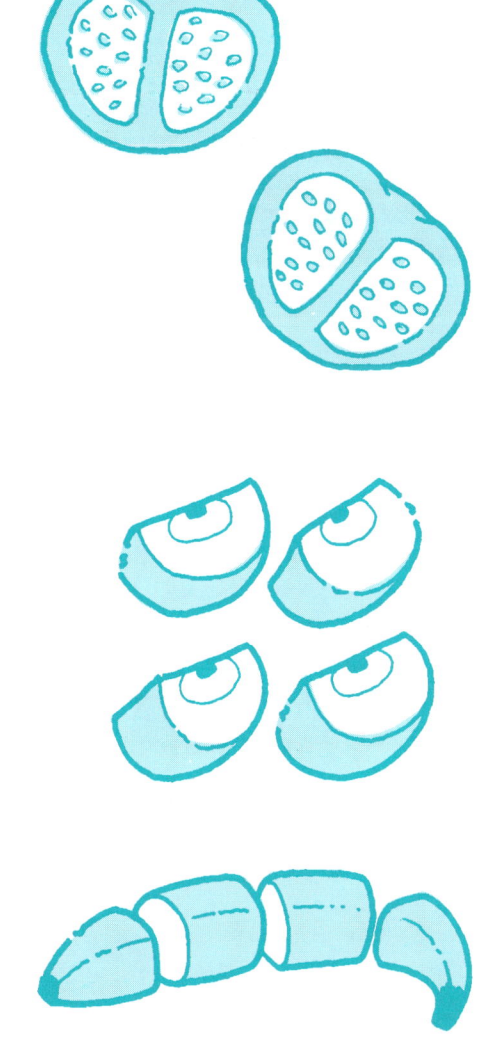

Now turn over

Divide each shape into four equal pieces. Use the dots to help you draw the lines. Then shade each of the four quarters in different colours.

Don't forget that equal fractions don't have to be the same shape but they must take up the same amount of space.

Can you find lots of different ways of dividing these rectangles into quarters? One has already been done for you.

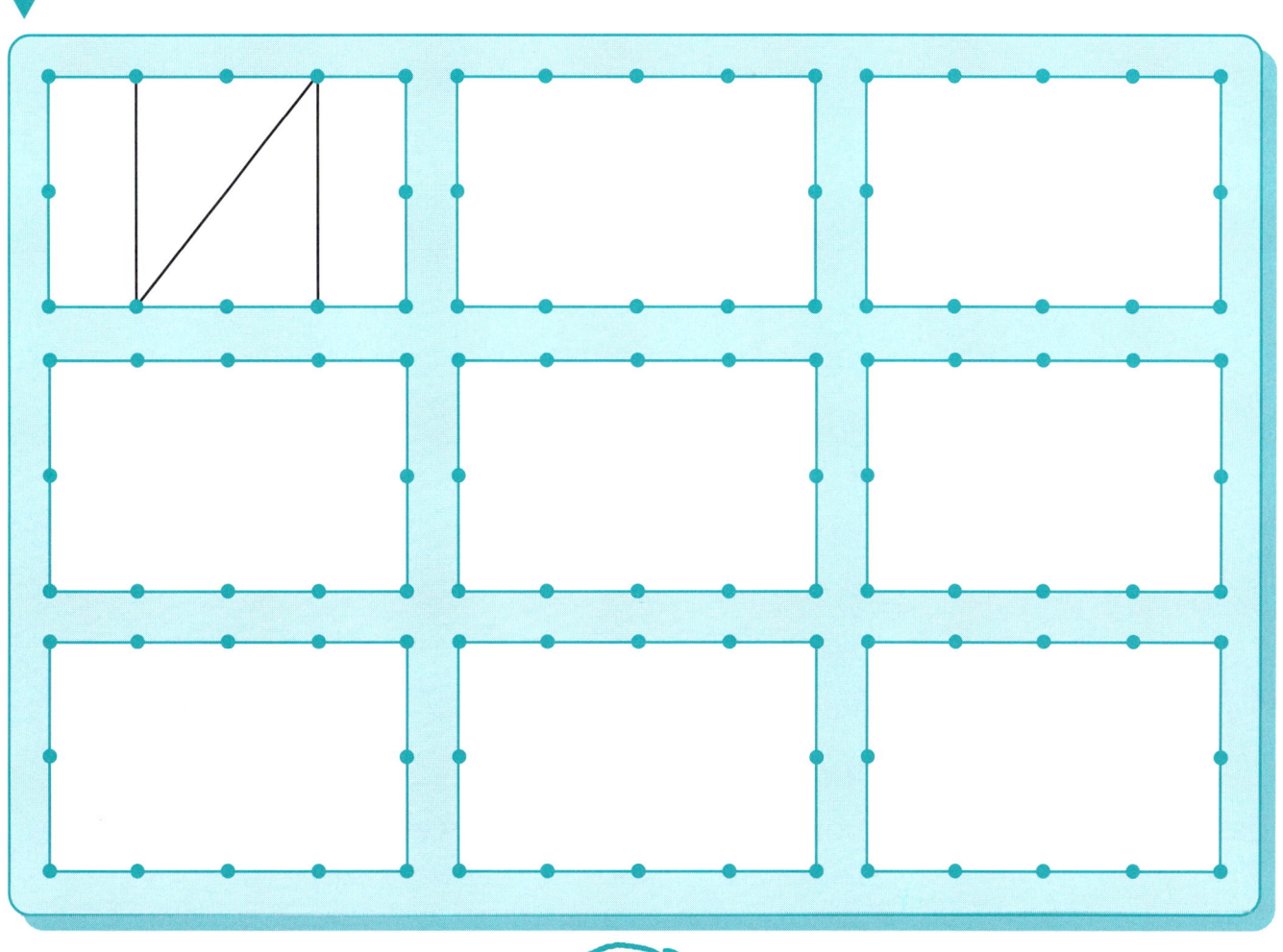

Can you spell these useful words?

fraction	
quarter	
divide	
half	
halves	
equal	

When you finish this step put a sticker here!

Dear Parent or Carer

This first step lays an important foundation for the work in the rest of the book. It is particularly important to stress the idea that a shape is *only* divided into halves or quarters when the pieces are in equal proportion. At first, your child may find it useful to think of halves and quarters as being of the same shape but, as the activity above demonstrates, this does not have to be the case. Answers on page 30.

Step 2: Introducing thirds

This step will help you to make and recognise shapes which are divided into thirds ($\frac{1}{3}$).

If you share something into three equal amounts each part is called a third ($\frac{1}{3}$).

Use the dots to split each of these shapes into three equal parts ($\frac{1}{3}$).

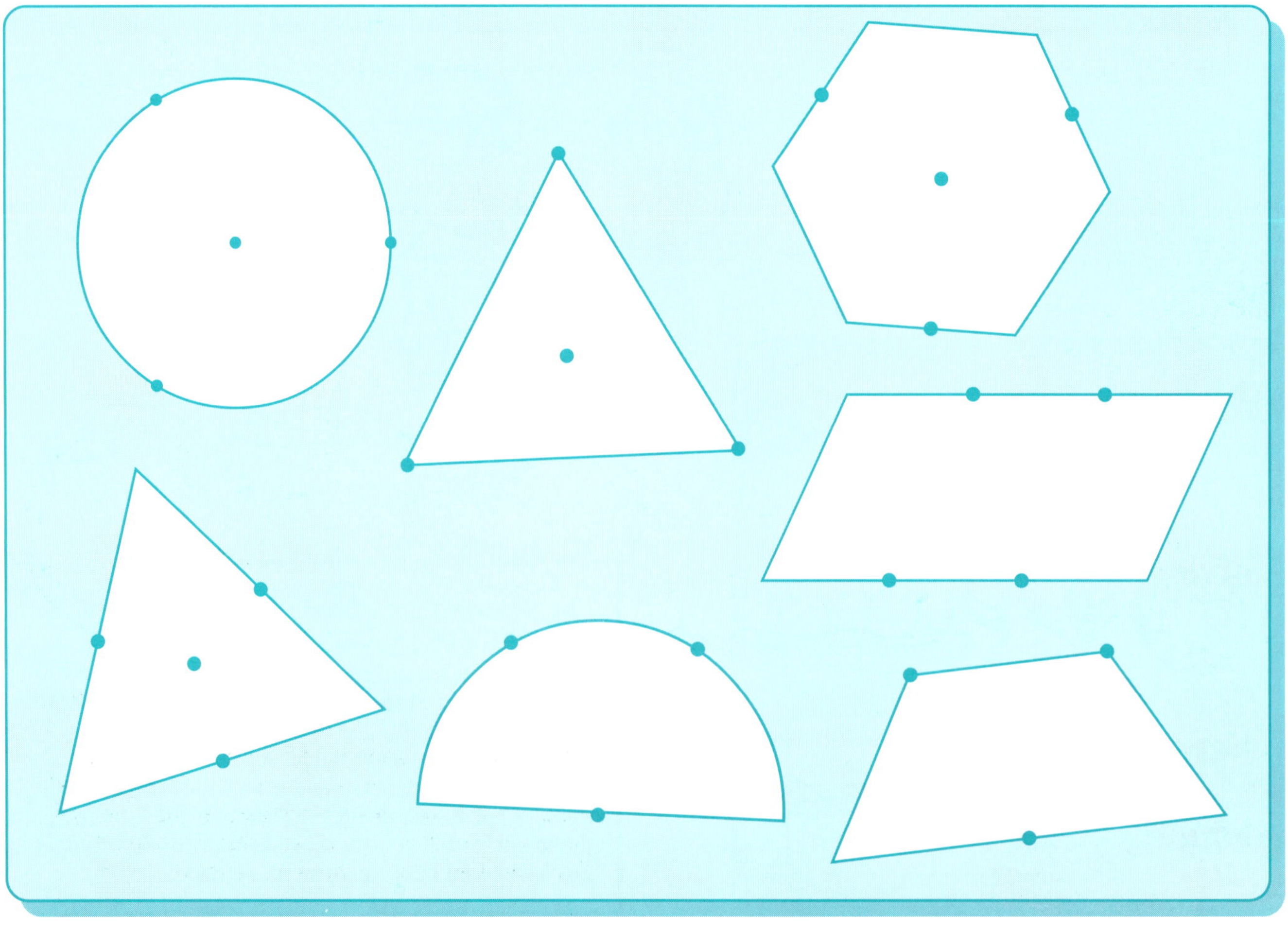

Colour one section of each shape and tick all those which are divided into thirds.

Dear Parent or Carer

Your child may be unfamiliar with the use of *one third* as it is not so widely experienced in everyday situations as halves and quarters. When deciding if shapes are split into thirds, you could talk to your child about whether the area of each piece is the same, you might also consider dividing and sharing food into three equal portions. Answers on page 30.

Step 3: Introducing eighths

This step will help you to make and recognise shapes which are divided into eighths ($\frac{1}{8}$).

Shade one eighth ($\frac{1}{8}$) of each of these shapes.
▼

If you share something into eight equal amounts we call those parts eighths.

Is one eighth of each shape below shaded? Mark each one with a ✓ or ✗.
▼

Can you find a different way to divide each of these squares into eighths?

You might want to copy these two examples. They may give you ideas for other ways.

When you finish this step put a sticker here!

Dear Parent or Carer

This step follows closely the ideas explored in Steps 1 and 2 on pages 2 and 6.
One eighth is a convenient fraction as it can be reached by repeatedly halving a whole shape to give two halves, four quarters, then eight eighths. Before working on through this book, check that your child recognises that a fraction relates to how much space is taken up, not just the number of pieces in a given shape. Answers on pages 30 and 31.

Step 4 — Introducing tenths

This step will help you to make and recognise shapes which are divided into tenths ($\frac{1}{10}$).

Shade one tenth ($\frac{1}{10}$) of each of these shapes.

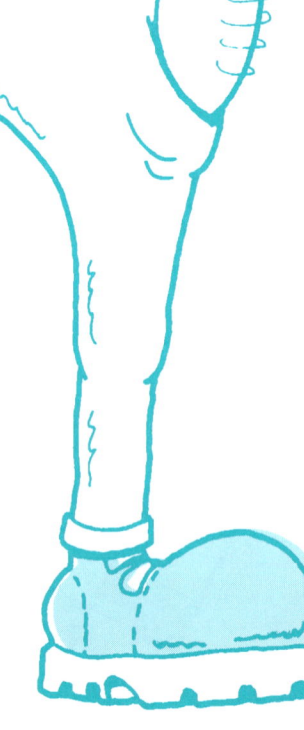

Sharing something into ten equal amounts gives us tenths. When we use decimals in money and measurement we are often working with tenths.

Look at these shapes. Is one tenth of each one shaded? Mark them with a ✓ or ✗.

For each pattern, colour in 9 out of every 10 tiles. When you have finished, you should have just one tenth left uncoloured in each one. Count the uncoloured shapes to complete the number statements.

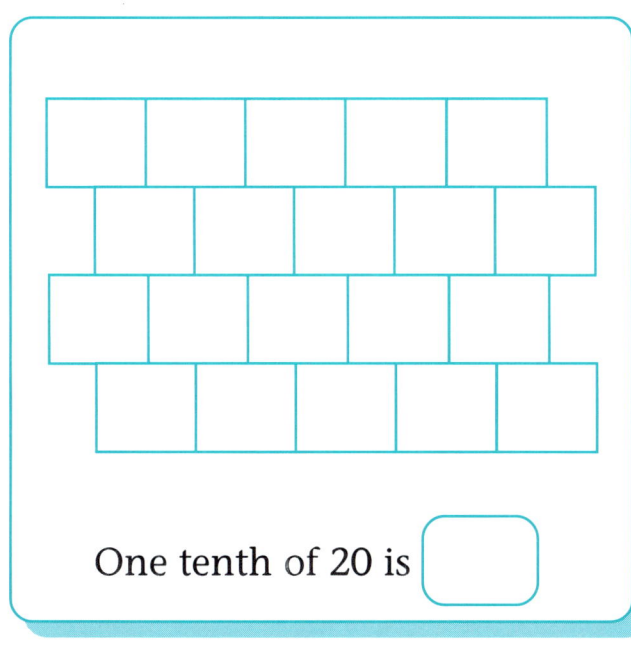

One tenth of 20 is ☐

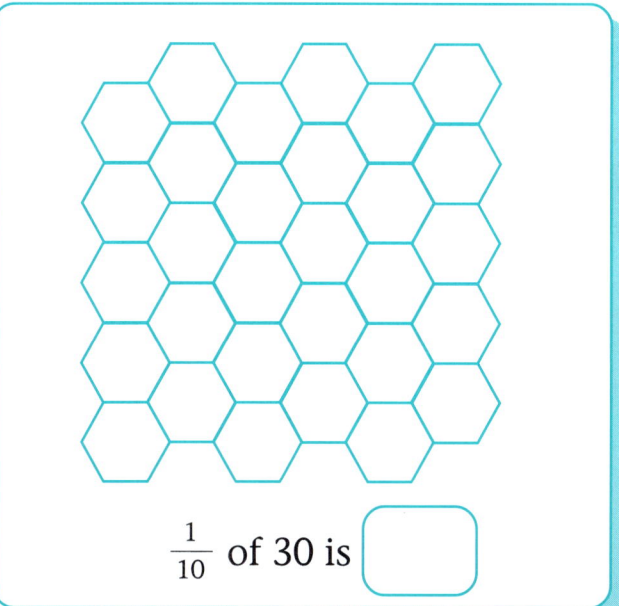

$\frac{1}{10}$ of 30 is ☐

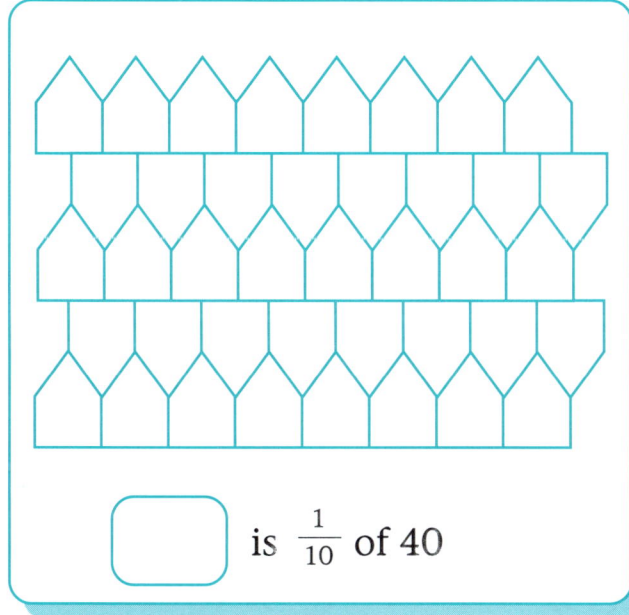

☐ is $\frac{1}{10}$ of 40

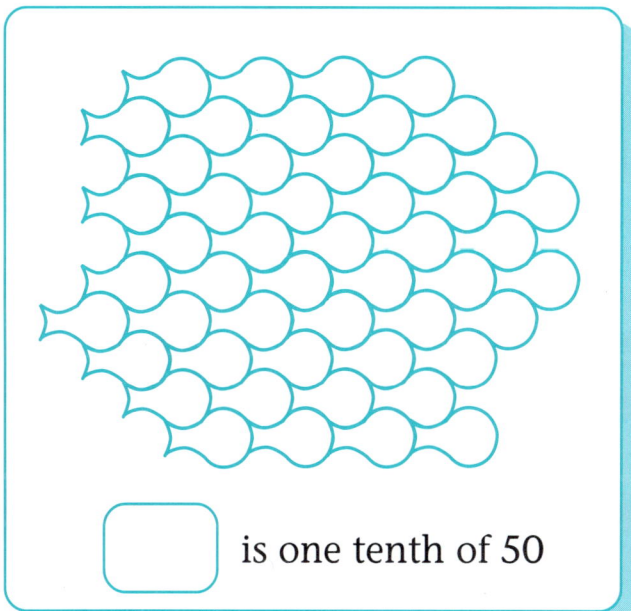

☐ is one tenth of 50

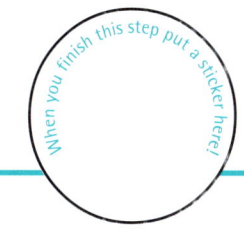

When you finish this step put a sticker here!

Dear Parent or Carer

Initially some young children think that one tenth is a fairly large fraction because it is based on 'ten'. This page will help to reinforce the idea that the more a shape is sub-divided, the smaller the fraction becomes. Answers on page 31.

Step 5

Halves and quarters of numbers

This step will help you to find half ($\frac{1}{2}$) and quarter ($\frac{1}{4}$) of a number. It will also introduce you to finding three quarters ($\frac{3}{4}$) of an amount.

Use a crayon to shade half of the squares in each snake.
▼

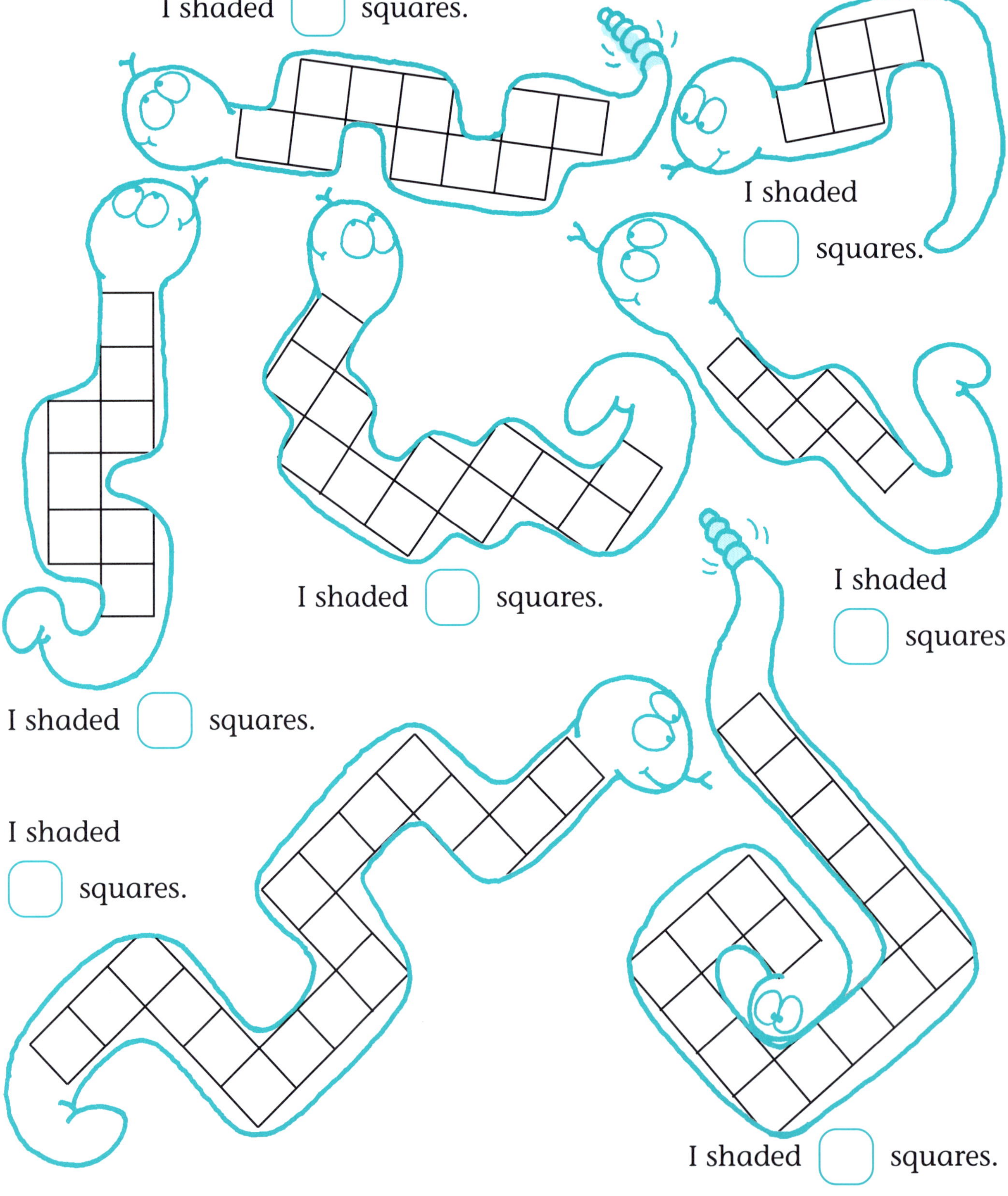

I shaded ☐ squares.

I shaded ☐ squares.

I shaded ☐ squares.

I shaded ☐ squares.

I shaded ☐ squares.

I shaded ☐ squares.

I shaded ☐ squares.

I shaded ☐ squares.

Shade one quarter of each shape and count the pieces to complete the number sentences.

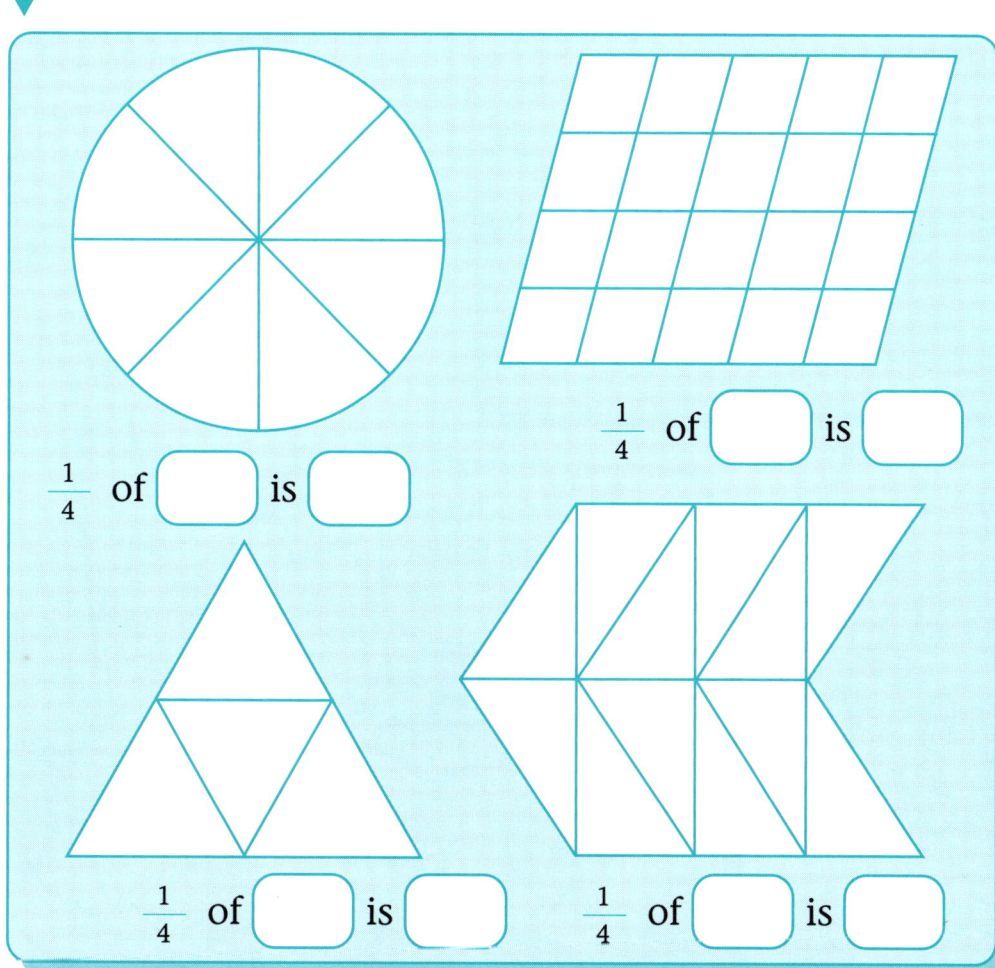

$\frac{1}{4}$ of ☐ is ☐

$\frac{1}{4}$ of ☐ is ☐

$\frac{1}{4}$ of ☐ is ☐

$\frac{1}{4}$ of ☐ is ☐

Find one quarter of these numbers by halving each one twice. The first one has been done for you.

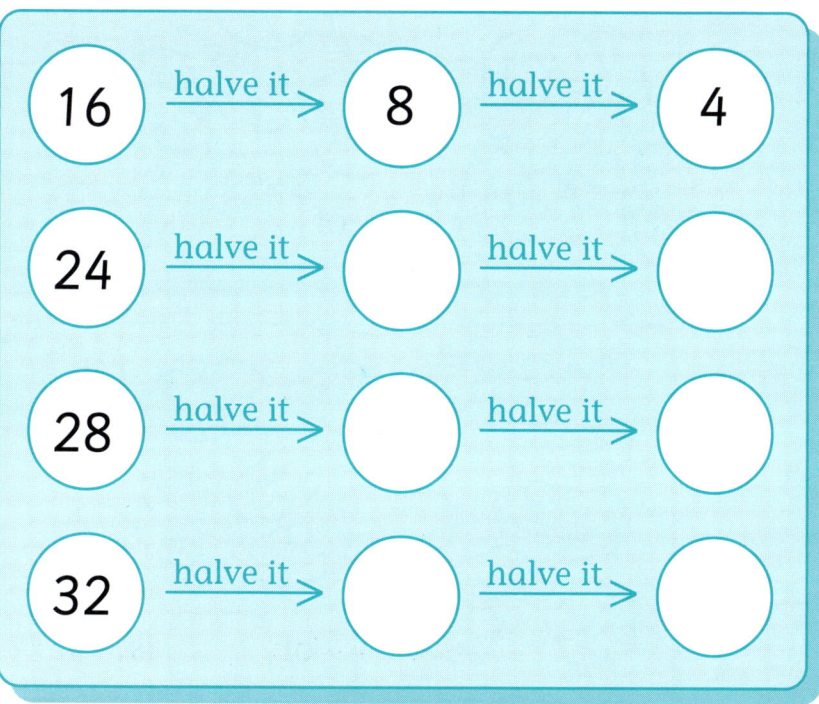

Now turn over

If you eat one quarter ($\frac{1}{4}$) of this chocolate bar, you will be left with three-quarters ($\frac{3}{4}$). This chocolate bar has 8 pieces. How many pieces in three-quarters?

▼

I work out one quarter of the number in the set and then treble it.

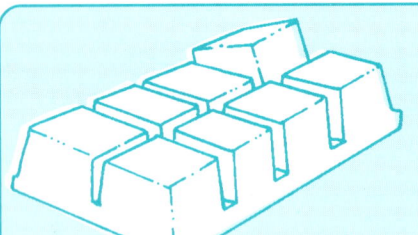

$\frac{1}{4}$ of ☐ is ☐

$\frac{3}{4}$ of ☐ is ☐

Shade $\frac{3}{4}$ of each set:

▼

I just shade three out of every four objects.

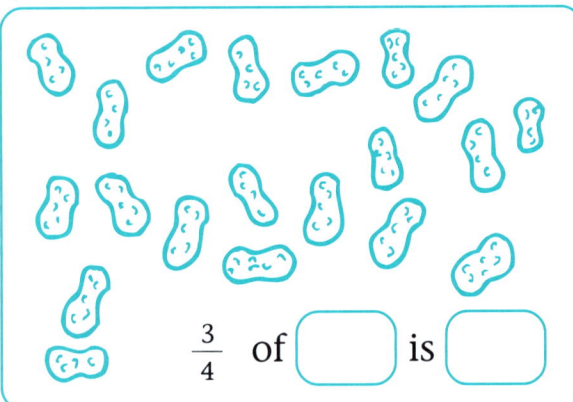

$\frac{3}{4}$ of ☐ is ☐

$\frac{3}{4}$ of ☐ is ☐

$\frac{3}{4}$ of ☐ is ☐

$\frac{3}{4}$ of ☐ is ☐

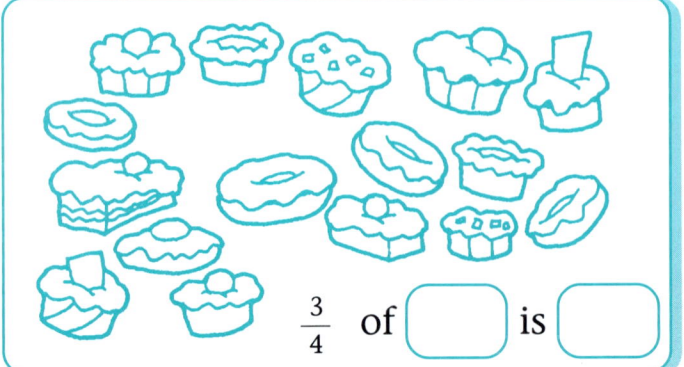

$\frac{3}{4}$ of ☐ is ☐

Which choice of food would give the animal more? Colour the better choice of food in each case.

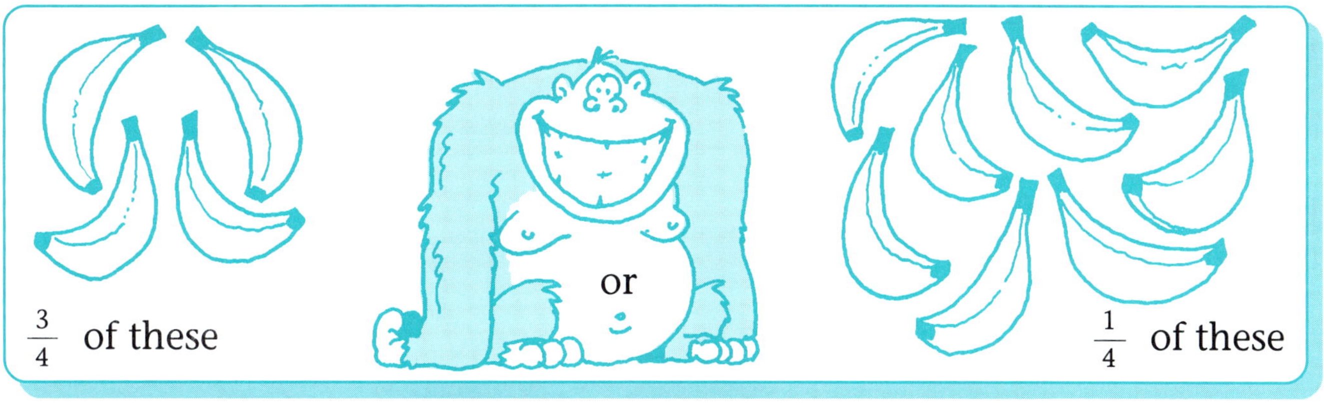

3/4 of these
or
1/4 of these

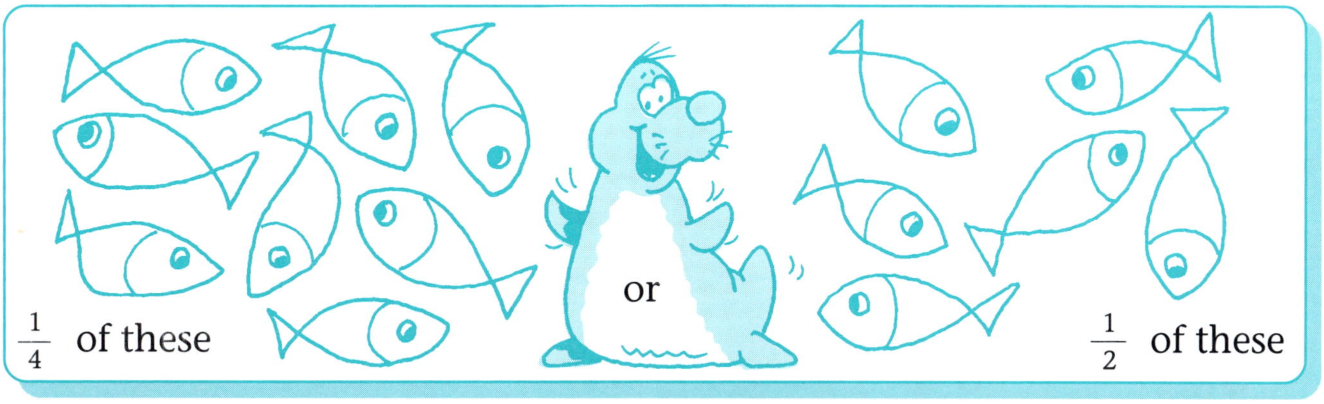

1/4 of these
or
1/2 of these

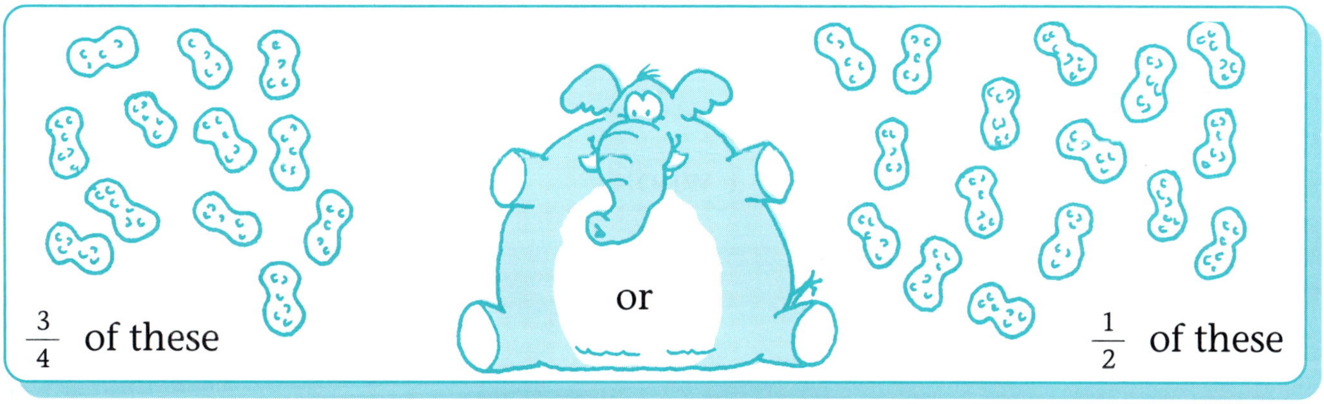

3/4 of these
or
1/2 of these

When you finish this step put a sticker here!

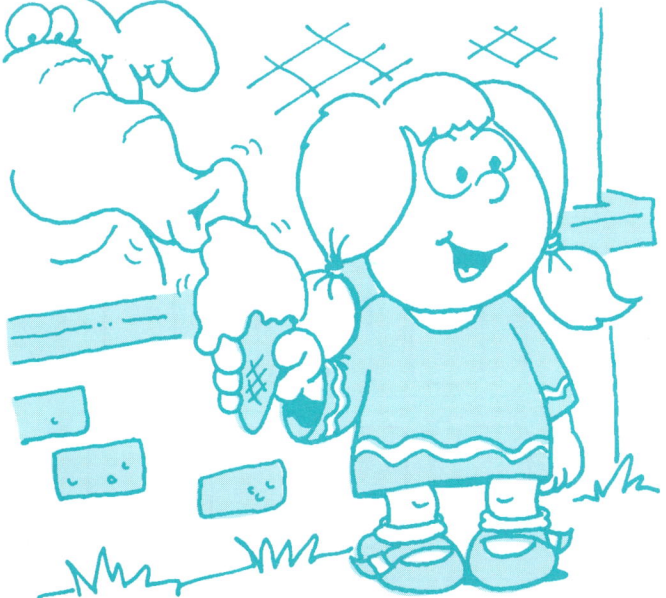

Dear Parent or Carer

This step extends the ideas introduced in Step 1 (page 2) by exploring halves and quarters of a number of objects as parts in a whole or as separated items in a set.
There are various ways of calculating $\frac{3}{4}$ of a quantity:

- find $\frac{1}{4}$ and triple that amount;
- find $\frac{1}{2}$, find $\frac{1}{4}$ and combine the two;
- pick three out of every four objects.

It is a good idea to talk to your child about the method he or she used to work out the answers to these questions. Answers on page 31.

Step 6: Same-sized pieces, different fractions

This step will help you to compare fractions of a whole.

Label this fraction wall using these symbols:

$\frac{1}{2}$, $\frac{1}{10}$, $\frac{1}{4}$, $\frac{1}{3}$, $\frac{1}{8}$

You can use the fraction wall to help you complete Step 6.

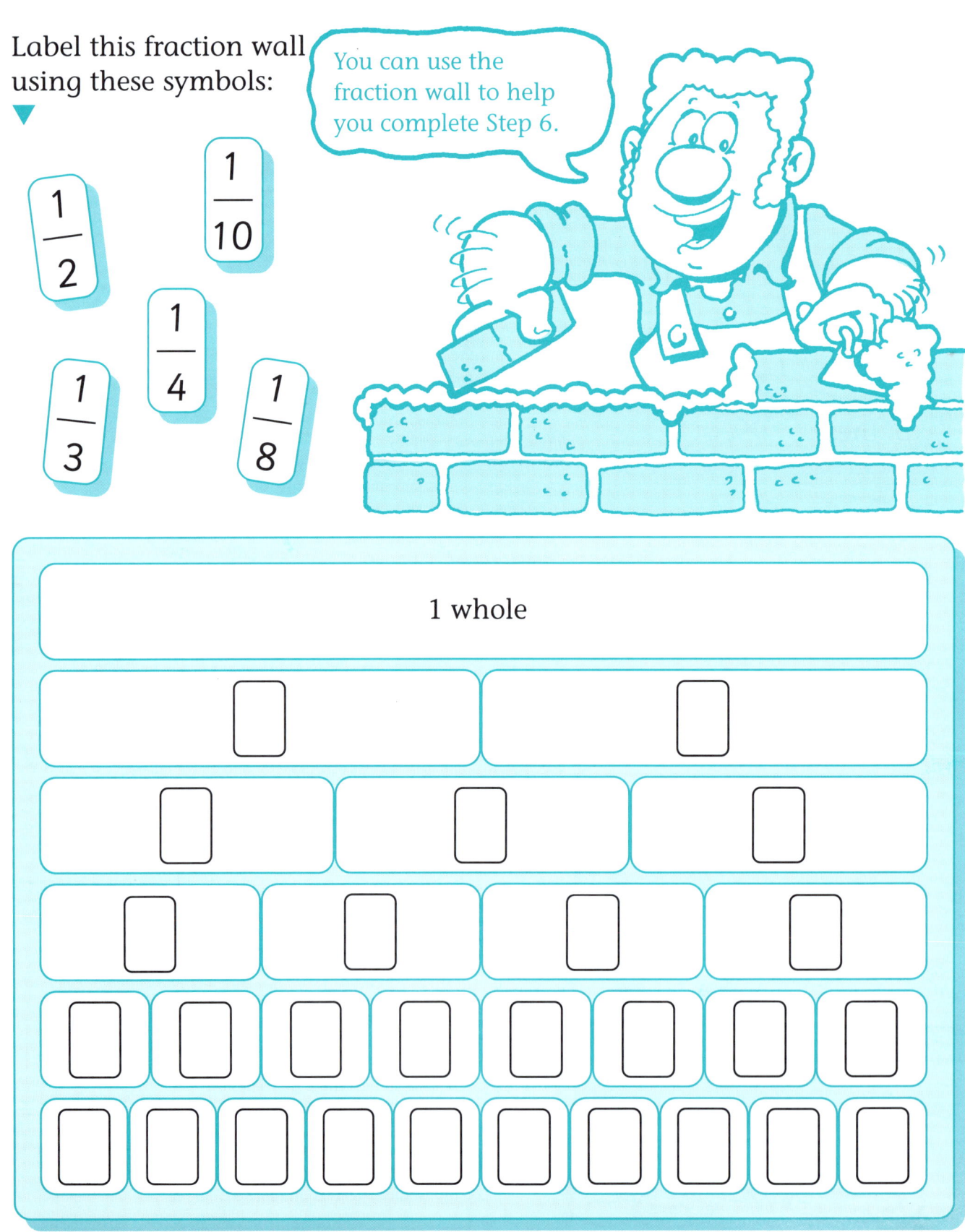

Can you match bricks of the same size? Shade any matching bricks with the same colour.

▼

Colour the larger of these fractions. One has been done to help you.

▼

Remember that fractions are about sharing equally. A fraction is always a part of a larger whole.

Now turn over

Don't forget! Use your fraction wall to help you.

Draw two arrows on each set of pictures.
An arrow means 'is greater than'.
▼

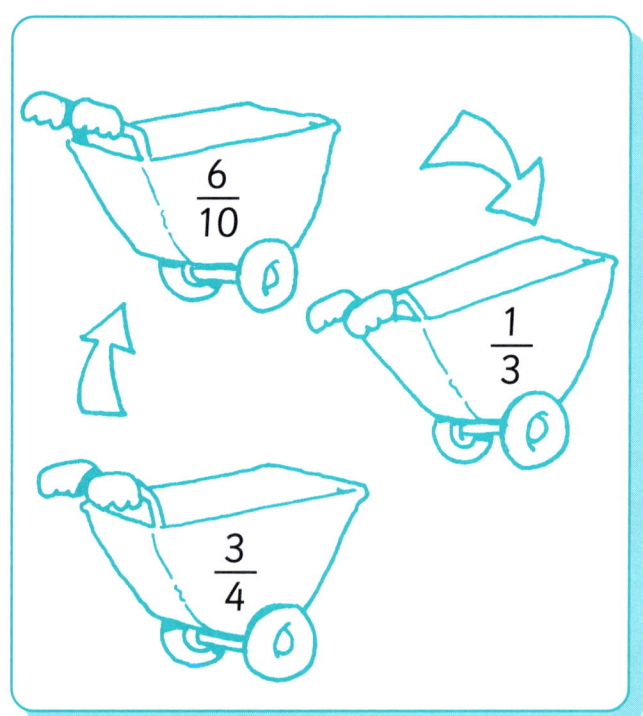

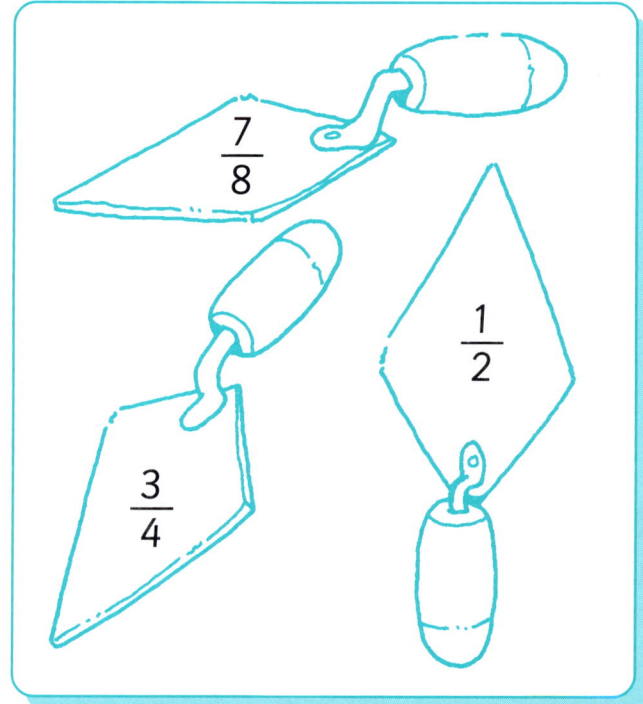

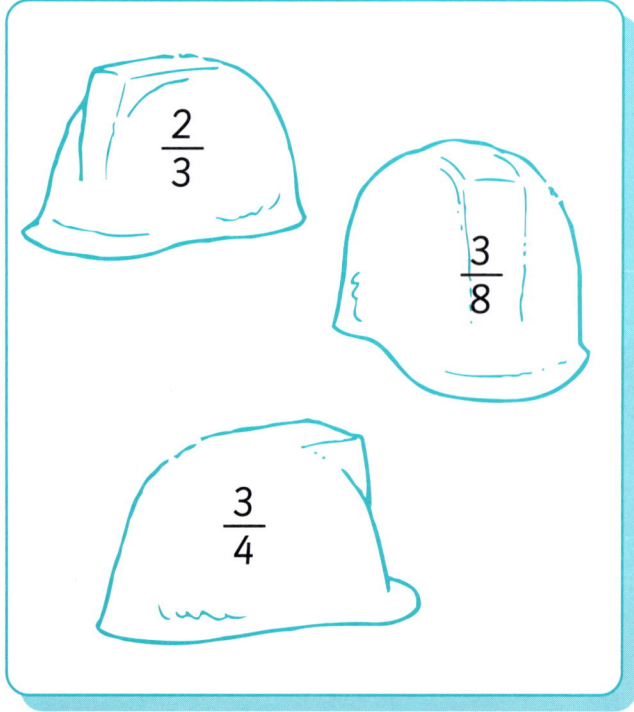

Use each of the numbers provided to make matching pairs of fractions, such as $\frac{1}{4} = \frac{2}{8}$. Try to find a different answer to the second example.

(Don't just copy your last answer!)

Dear Parent or Carer

When two fractions have the same value but are written in different forms (such as $\frac{1}{2}$ and $\frac{4}{8}$) these are called 'equivalent fractions'.
All the work in this step can be supported by using the fraction wall on page 16. However, your child may start to recognise how the number relationships work ($\frac{1}{2} \rightarrow$ multiply both numbers by $5 \rightarrow \frac{5}{10}$). Answers on page 31.

Step 7: Using fractions

This step will help you to add fractions.

You can use this fraction wheel to compare and to combine fractions. Colour the number wheel and label the fractions.
▼

$\frac{1}{2}$

Look at the largest piece on the wheel. Can you see that you would need four of the smallest pieces, or two of the middle-sized pieces, to make another piece the same?

Now use your number wheel to add and take away these fractions.

$\frac{1}{2} + \frac{1}{2} =$ ☐ $\frac{1}{2} + \frac{1}{4} =$ ☐

$\frac{1}{2} + \frac{1}{8} + \frac{1}{8} =$ ☐ $\frac{1}{4} + \frac{1}{4} =$ ☐

$\frac{1}{2} + \frac{1}{4} + \frac{1}{8} =$ ☐ $\frac{1}{4} + \frac{1}{8} =$ ☐

$\frac{1}{8} + \frac{1}{8} + \frac{1}{4} =$ ☐ $\frac{1}{2} + \frac{1}{8} =$ ☐

$\frac{1}{4} + \frac{1}{4} + \frac{1}{8} =$ ☐ $\frac{1}{8} + \frac{1}{8} =$ ☐

$\frac{1}{2} - \frac{1}{4} =$ ☐ $1 - \frac{1}{2} =$ ☐

$\frac{1}{4} - \frac{1}{8} =$ ☐ $1 - \frac{1}{4} =$ ☐

$1 - \frac{1}{8} =$ ☐ $\frac{1}{2} - \frac{1}{8} =$ ☐

Now turn over

How many ways can you make a total of 1? One fraction sum has been done for you.

$\frac{1}{2} + \frac{1}{4} + \frac{1}{4} = 1$

Complete these fraction sums using the numbers provided.

$\dfrac{1}{\Box} + \dfrac{1}{\Box} = \dfrac{3}{\Box}$ 4, 2, 4

$\dfrac{1}{\Box} + \dfrac{\Box}{8} = \dfrac{5}{\Box}$ 8, 2, 1

$\dfrac{3}{\Box} + \dfrac{1}{\Box} = \dfrac{5}{\Box}$ 4, 8, 8

$\dfrac{3}{\Box} + \dfrac{3}{\Box} = \dfrac{3}{\Box}$ 8, 4, 8

$\dfrac{1}{\Box} + \dfrac{1}{\Box} = \dfrac{\Box}{\Box}$ 3, 8, 8, 4

$\dfrac{2}{\Box} + \dfrac{1}{\Box} = \dfrac{\Box}{\Box}$ 1, 8, 2, 4

Dear Parent or Carer

This step introduces the idea of adding fractions. At this stage there is no need for your child to be able to convert fractions from one form to another, providing he or she continues to refer to the number wheel on page 20.
Eventually your child will be taught the precise vocabulary of fractions:
$1 \leftarrow$ numerator
$\overline{4} \leftarrow$ denominator
Answers on pages 31 and 32.

When you finish this step put a sticker here!

Step 8: Introducing mixed numbers

This step will show you how to write and add fractions beyond the value of 1.

Write in the missing numbers on these lines.

Number lines aren't just for whole numbers! With these number lines you need to look at the points between whole numbers to work out which fractions you need to fill in.

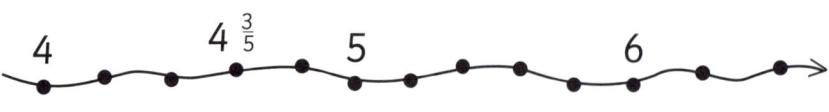

Remember that number lines can be for fractions as well as whole numbers!

Now make your own fraction number line.

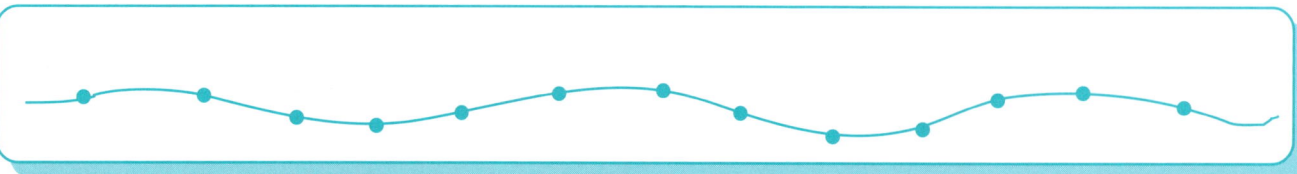

Look at the example below. It will help you to add these mixed numbers.

▼

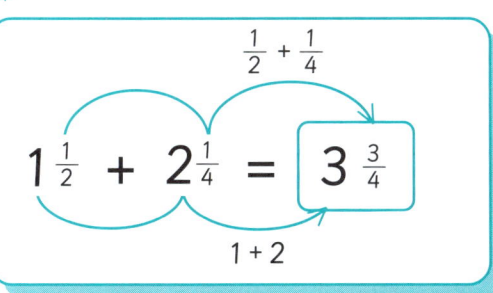

Remember the number wheel:

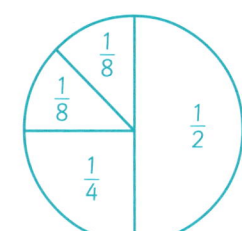

$\frac{4}{8} = \frac{1}{2}$ and $\frac{2}{4} = \frac{1}{2}$ and $\frac{1}{4} = \frac{2}{8}$, and so on.

$3\frac{1}{4} + 2\frac{1}{4} =$ ☐

$4\frac{1}{8} + 3\frac{1}{4} =$ ☐

$1\frac{3}{4} + 2\frac{1}{8} =$ ☐

$4\frac{3}{8} + 4\frac{1}{8} =$ ☐

$3\frac{5}{8} + 2\frac{1}{4} =$ ☐

$2\frac{3}{8} + 1\frac{1}{4} =$ ☐

Use this space to write some of your own!

▼

When you finish this step put a sticker here!

Dear Parent or Carer

It is important to recognise that fractions go beyond the idea of the 'single unit'.
Your child does not, at this stage, need to be able to convert fractions to a common denominator, for example making all into halves or tenths, when adding, but may continue to use the fraction wall on page 16 or the fraction wheel on page 20. Answers on page 32.

Step 9

Introducing decimals

This step will introduce you to decimals as part of a whole unit, and decimals along a number line.

Shade the fractions shown. The first one has been done for you.

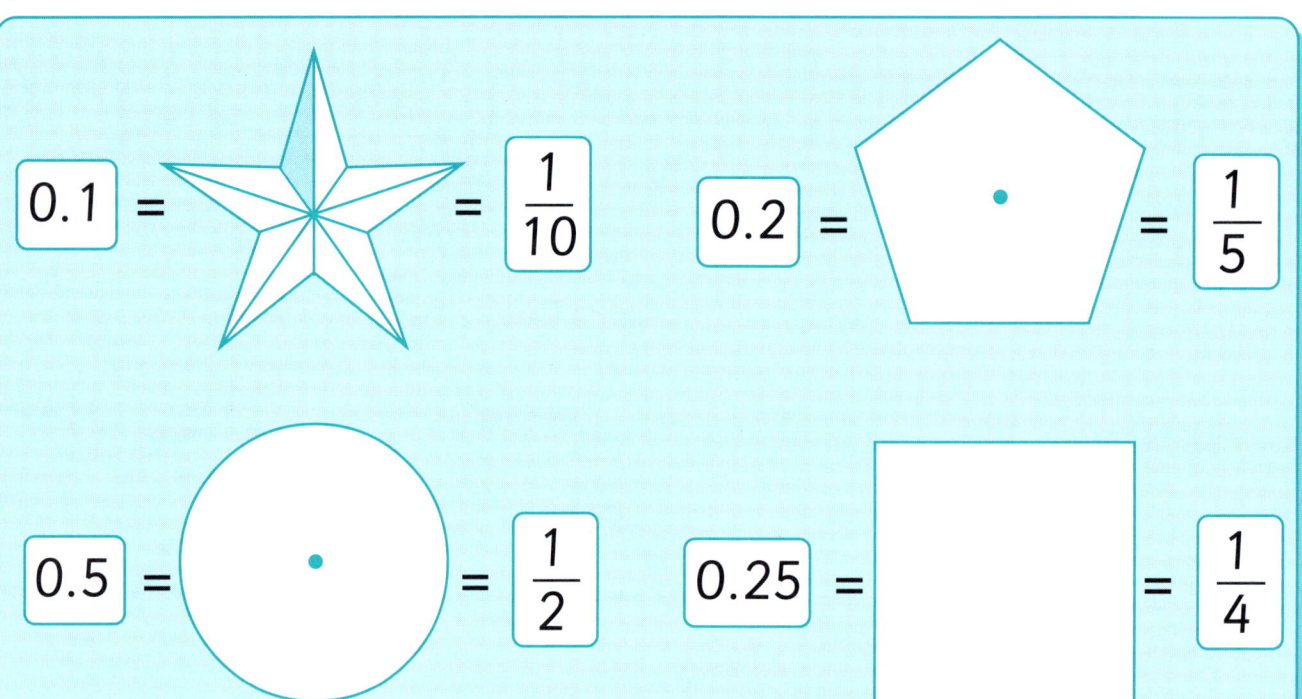

Just as we count in hundreds, tens and ones, our decimal system allows us to count parts of a 1 in tenths and hundredths.

The **decimal point** shows where the whole ones finish and the parts start. We can also divide each tenth into ten parts – these are called hundredths.

Complete these number lines.

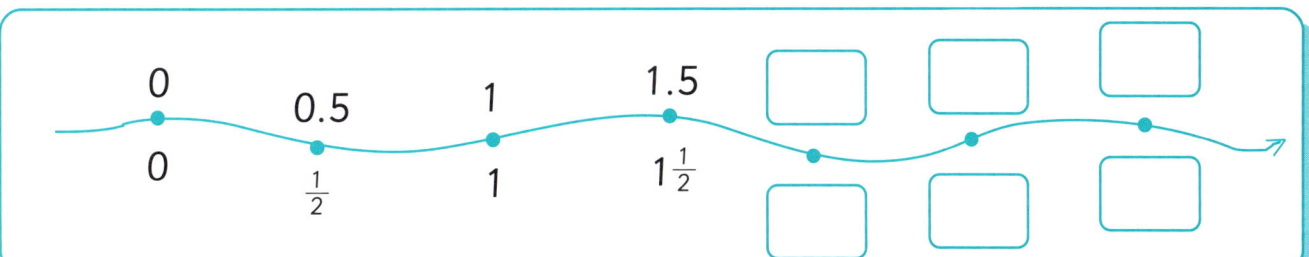

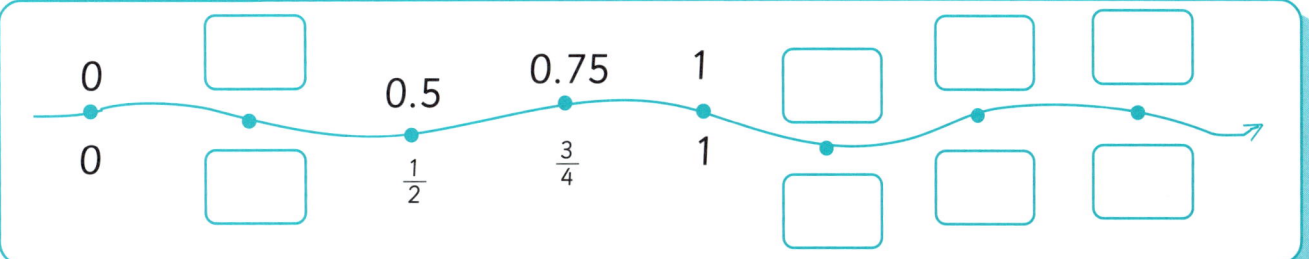

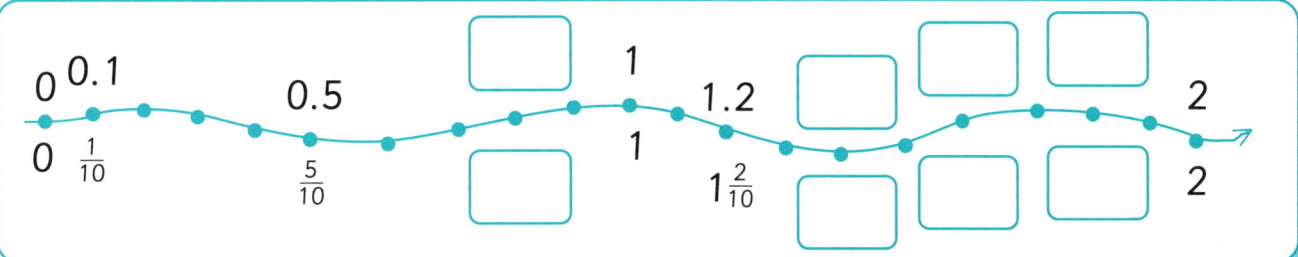

Use your number lines to write the following fractions as decimals.

Dear Parent or Carer

Fractions are all around us, so it is important that your child has a solid understanding of what they are about. Take any opportunity to point out examples of the use of fractions in everyday life, such as:
- sharing money (£5 between two is £2 $\frac{1}{2}$ which is £2.50);
- cooking (scaling quantities in a recipe up or down to cater for different numbers of people);
- shopping (knowing whether it is better value to buy a more expensive box of cereal which weighs 750g or a cheaper box which only weighs 500g).

Answers on page 32.

Step 10 Using decimals

This step will help you to add and order decimals.

Convert these fractions into decimals and then add them. The first one has been done for you.
▼

$\frac{1}{2} + \frac{1}{2} =$ | 0.5 | + | 0.5 | = | 1.0

$\frac{1}{10} + \frac{1}{10} =$ ☐ + ☐ = ☐

$\frac{1}{2} + \frac{1}{10} =$ ☐ + ☐ = ☐

$\frac{1}{4} + \frac{1}{4} =$ ☐ + ☐ = ☐

$\frac{1}{4} + \frac{1}{2} =$ ☐ + ☐ = ☐

$\frac{3}{4} + \frac{1}{4} =$ ☐ + ☐ = ☐

Can you remember everything you learned before?

$\frac{2}{4} = \frac{1}{2}$ $\frac{1}{2} = 0.5$

$\frac{2}{8} = \frac{1}{4}$ $\frac{1}{10} = 0.1$

$\frac{6}{8} = \frac{3}{4}$ $\frac{1}{4} = 0.25$

Use these numbers to make lots of different totals:

▼

| 0.4 | 0.25 | 0.75 | 0.5 |

0.5 + 0.25 ───── 0.75	+	+
+	+	+

Write your answers in order, from smallest to largest, in the space below.

▼

Dear Parent or Carer

Your child should be made aware that decimal fractions need to be set out carefully for adding (see example top left), just as with adding tens and units. The first digit after the decimal point represents tenths, the second digit represents hundredths. At this stage however, your child should only be expected to calculate and compare simple decimal fractions. Answers on page 32.

When you finish this step put a sticker here!

Parents' pages

 Step 1: Introducing halves and quarters

Page 2: The shapes are simply split through the middle. Some shapes, such as the square and hexagon (6 sides), can be divided in more than one way.
e.g.

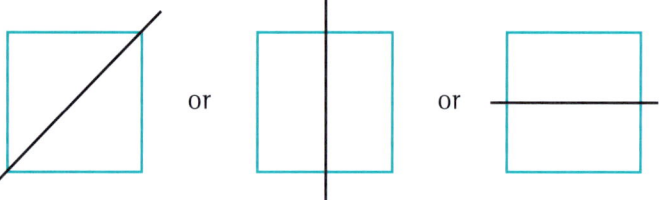

Page 3: Some possible solutions include those shown below. The remainder must also pass through the centre of the square.

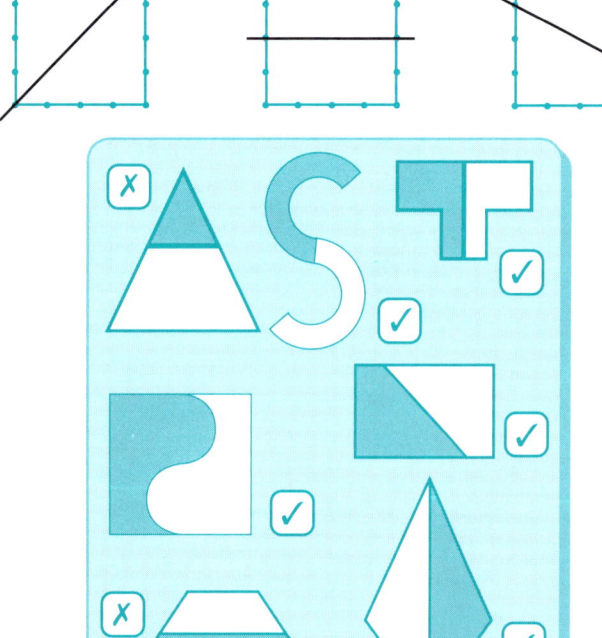

Page 4:

Page 5: Some possible solutions include:

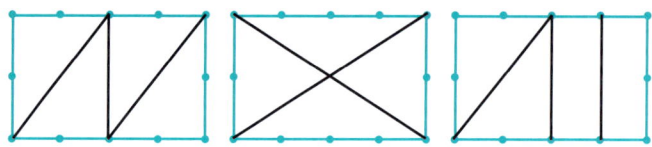

 Step 2: Introducing thirds

Page 6:

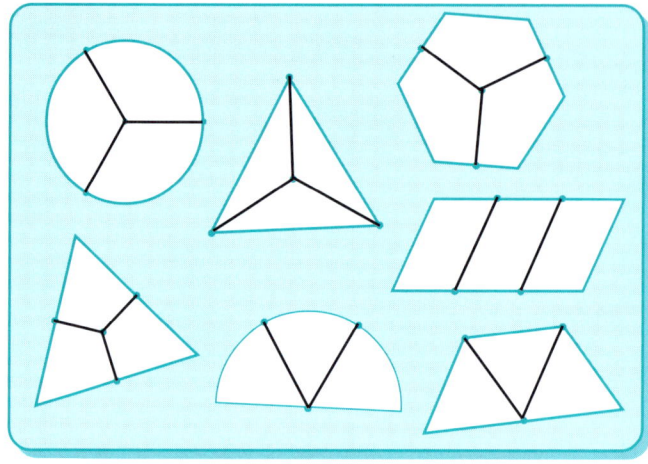

Page 7: One section of each shape should be coloured.

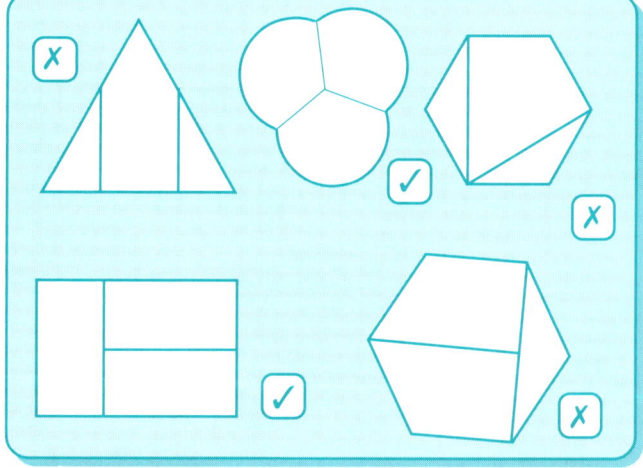

 Step 3: Introducing eighths

Page 8: Each shape in the upper part of the page will have one segment/portion shaded.

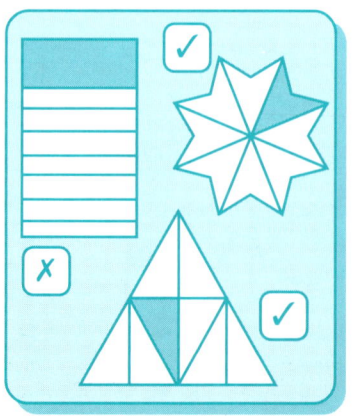

Page 9: Some possible solutions include:

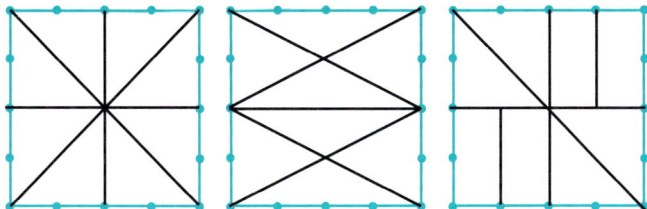

 Step 4 : Introducing tenths

Page 10: Each shape in the upper part of the page will have one segment/portion shaded.

Page 11: One tenth of 20 is 2; $\frac{1}{10}$ of 30 is 3; 4 is $\frac{1}{10}$ of 40; 5 is one tenth of 50.

 Step 5: Halves and quarters of numbers

Page 12:

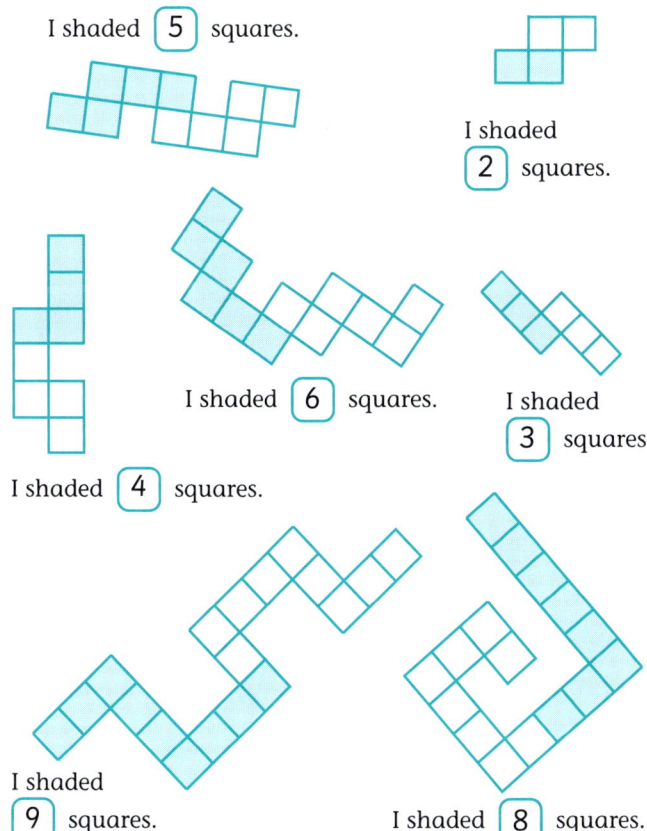

Page 13: $\frac{1}{4}$ of 8 is 2; $\frac{1}{4}$ of 20 is 5; $\frac{1}{4}$ of 4 is 1; $\frac{1}{4}$ of 12 is 3. 16, 8, 4; 24, 12, 6; 28, 14, 7; 32, 16, 8.

Page 14: $\frac{1}{4}$ of 8 is 2; $\frac{3}{4}$ of 8 is 6. $\frac{3}{4}$ of 20 is 15; $\frac{3}{4}$ of 4 is 3; $\frac{3}{4}$ of 12 is 9; $\frac{3}{4}$ of 8 is 6; $\frac{3}{4}$ of 16 is 12.

Page 15: 3 or 2 bananas; 2 or 3 fish; 9 or 8 peanuts.

 Step 6: Same-sized pieces, different fractions

Page 16:

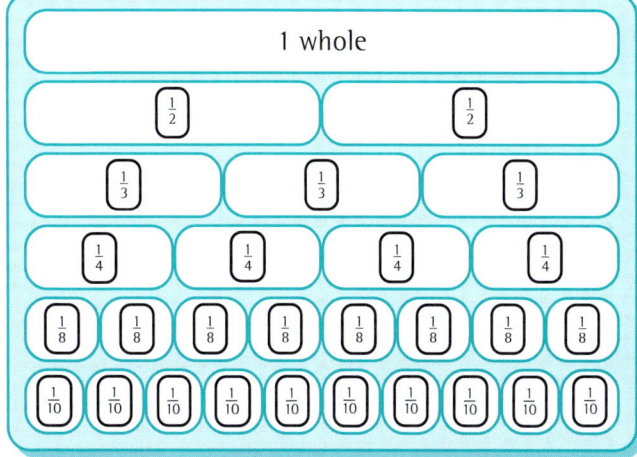

Page 17: $\frac{1}{2}, \frac{5}{10}, \frac{4}{8}$ and $\frac{2}{4}$; $\frac{3}{4}$ and $\frac{6}{8}$; $\frac{1}{4}$ and $\frac{2}{8}$. $\frac{7}{8}$ is larger than $\frac{3}{4}$; $\frac{3}{4}$ is larger than $\frac{2}{3}$; $\frac{1}{2}$ is larger than $\frac{1}{3}$; $\frac{3}{8}$ is larger than $\frac{1}{3}$; $\frac{1}{4}$ is larger than $\frac{2}{10}$.

Page 18: $\frac{7}{8} \to \frac{3}{4} \to \frac{1}{2}$; $\frac{3}{4} \to \frac{2}{3} \to \frac{3}{8}$; $\frac{3}{8} \to \frac{3}{10} \to \frac{1}{4}$.

Page 19: $\frac{1}{2} = \frac{5}{10}$; $\frac{1}{2} = \frac{4}{8}$; $\frac{3}{4} = \frac{6}{8}$; $\frac{3}{6} = \frac{4}{8}$; $\frac{1}{2} = \frac{2}{4}$; $\frac{1}{3} = \frac{2}{6}$.

 Step 7: Using fractions

Page 20:

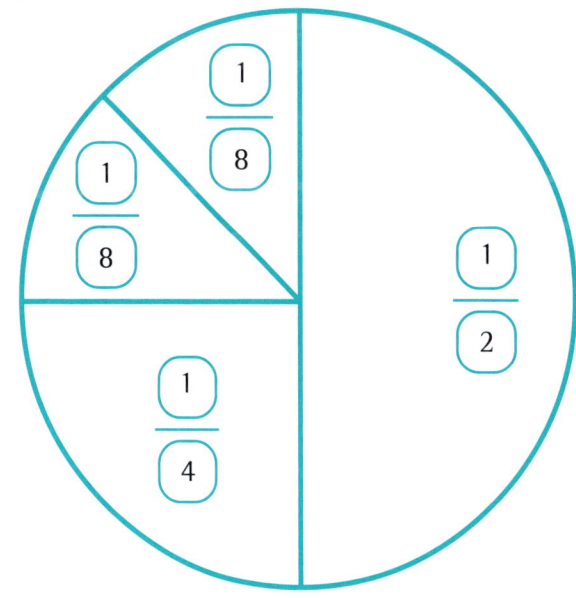

Page 21: $\frac{1}{2} + \frac{1}{2} = 1$; $\frac{1}{2} + \frac{1}{4} = \frac{3}{4}$; $\frac{1}{2} + \frac{1}{8} + \frac{1}{8} = \frac{3}{4}$; $\frac{1}{4} + \frac{1}{4} = \frac{1}{2}$; $\frac{1}{2} + \frac{1}{4} + \frac{1}{8} = \frac{7}{8}$; $\frac{1}{4} + \frac{1}{8} = \frac{3}{8}$; $\frac{1}{8} + \frac{1}{8} + \frac{1}{4} = \frac{1}{2}$; $\frac{1}{2} + \frac{1}{8} = \frac{5}{8}$; $\frac{1}{4} + \frac{1}{4} + \frac{1}{8} = \frac{5}{8}$; $\frac{1}{8} + \frac{1}{8} = \frac{1}{4}$.
$\frac{1}{2} - \frac{1}{4} = \frac{1}{4}$; $1 - \frac{1}{2} = \frac{1}{2}$; $\frac{1}{4} - \frac{1}{8} = \frac{1}{8}$; $1 - \frac{1}{4} = \frac{3}{4}$; $1 - \frac{1}{8} = \frac{7}{8}$; $\frac{1}{2} - \frac{1}{8} = \frac{3}{8}$.

Page 22: Any combinations which total 1 unit are allowed. Subtraction is also allowed (e.g. $1\frac{1}{2} - \frac{1}{2}$).

Page 23:

 Step 8: Introducing mixed numbers

Page 24:

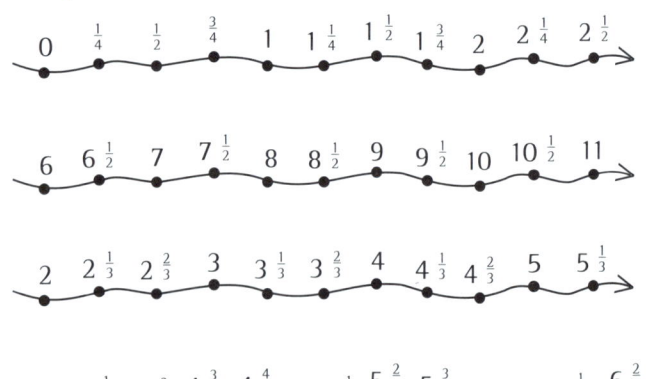

Page 25:

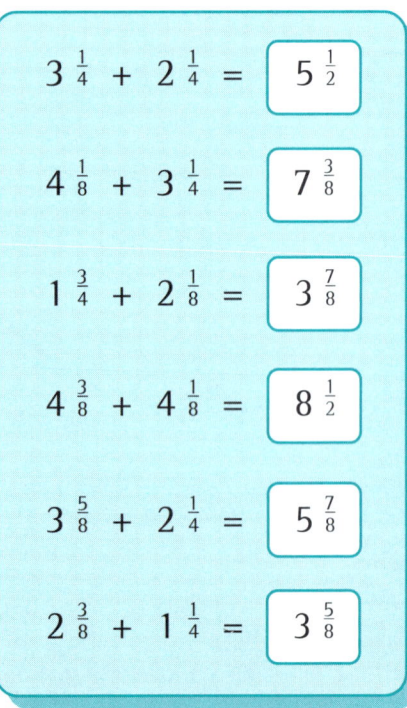

 Step 9: Introducing decimals

Page 26: Some possible solutions:

Page 27:

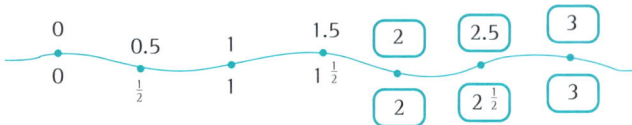

$\frac{3}{4} = 0.75$; $\frac{1}{10} = 0.1$; $\frac{9}{10} = 0.9$; $1\frac{1}{2} = 1.5$; $\frac{5}{10} = 0.5$; $1\frac{1}{4} = 1.25$.

 Step 10: Using decimals

Page 28:

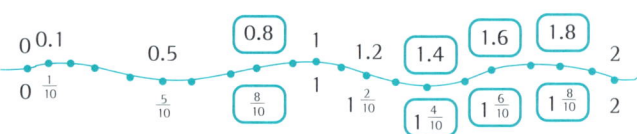

Page 29: Solutions are:

0.4	0.5	0.5	0.25	0.4	0.5
+0.25	+0.25	+0.4	+0.75	+0.75	+0.75
0.65	0.75	0.9	1.00	1.15	1.25